D0907153

Volume 82 of the Yale Series of Younger Poets

Julie Agoos

Above the Land

Foreword by James Merrill

Yale University Press
New Haven and London

Published with assistance from
the Mary Cady Tew Memorial Fund.

Designed by Sally Harris
and set in Monotype Bembo type by
the Anthoensen Press, Portland, Maine.
Printed in the United States of America by
the Alpine Press, Inc., Stoughton, Massachusetts.

Library of Congress Cataloging-in-Publication Data

Agoos, Julie, 1956–
  Above the land.

  (Yale series of younger poets ; v. 82)
  I. Title. II. Series.
PS3551.G59A64 1987   811'.54   86–26675
ISBN 0–300–03861–5 (alk. paper)
ISBN 0–300–03862–3 (pbk. : alk. paper)

The paper in this book meets the guidelines for
permanence and durability of the Committee on
Production Guidelines for Book Longevity
of the Council on Library Resources.

10 9 8 7 6 5 4 3 2 1

for my mother and father

Contents

Foreword

"So much sensation is unknown," writes Julie Agoos, and proceeds to challenge the sorry state of affairs:

> On the banks of that river that parts the city
> of Florence, should you straddle the wall,
> your pink legs will glow in twilight,
> hair fan up against the iron lampposts . . .

It's a "you" we recognize at once—the updated Henry James heroine savoring her Italy from an uncommitted vantage not thinkable to the local adult population.

Poets needn't travel. Look at Emily Dickinson. Look at Marianne Moore, who got more from a single issue of *The London Illustrated News* than Mother did from her entire junior year abroad. And yet, if travel is in the cards, Italy may still be its most reliable object. To see why, we should first ask, as Henry James never stopped doing, what claim the forms of art can possibly exert upon a writer with the usual blurred American perception of the forms of life. What have the look and speech and manners of our hometowns—settled only a few centuries ago by a fanatic sect or a shipload of criminals—in common with Parma's or Fiesole's age-old ways of doing and saying, just as effective in the pruning of trees as they are about to be in the seduction of that Lit major reading her guidebook at the café table? (Where better than Italy, for that matter, do we find writ large the offenses that comprise so much of the small print of American politics?) Until the forms of life are clearly felt, the forms of art will mean little. At best those we call "organic"—like fertilizer—may blaze in a master's hands. But Italy *teaches*. Here are the proportions that ease the heart, the images agleam with use, the spoken phrases of a fluency so natural that we forget how we distrusted it back home, where to grope for words proved our utter sincerity. In short, the poet straddling the wall may return to America thinking:

> It will have been worth something to have
> connected that life to your own existence.

Agoos makes her connections, and uses those foreign ways, as directly or obliquely as she pleases. "Porto Venere" is a distillation of impressions not unlike Browning's "Englishman in Italy," but with the feelings volatized out of sight. A more complex and ambitious piece, "An Afternoon's Activity," has two middle-aged women arriving exhausted in an Italian town—Florence? After lunch they part for a few hours. Diana, unwell, takes to bed with her dictionary, bent on learning and whenever possible using the numerous words prefixed by *porta-* (denoting what bears or contains, as in porter or portfolio, but also by itself the noun for door). Her friend goes for a walk, idly planning a card or letter to Diana's son at home. By the poem's end the Italian words are everywhere, the mother is even addressing her son *in* Italian. Doors, too, have proliferated—after all, in the beginning was the word for them. "Are these the doors to Paradise?" wonders Diana, early on. No, to a restaurant. But the question has been asked. Presently above certain doors appear terracotta plaques of the Madonna and Child, as do, in the appropriately italic inner monologues which edge the poem's action, some discreet sacramental images—oil, linen, wine. Thanks to a happy homophone, the absent son is balanced by "The sun in my lap as I try writing this postcard," and the card, whether written or not, merges with Diana's invocation to him as the doorkeeper to her very life:

> *Ma spero che stia*
> *in ogni caso*
> *alle porte*
> *quando arrivano*
> *queste lettere,*
> *quando arriverò,*
> *e quando vado via.*

Risky, that shift into Italian. Not all readers have a second language. Those who do, however, will recall times when they resorted to it for complicity ("Pas devant les enfants") as well as respite from the ready dramatics of the mother tongue. Both motives are at work here, for the poem's mother needs to spare her son—and herself— depths that might otherwise be too bluntly sounded. A similar tact informs the poem's "Christianity," which lacks the dead dogmatic weight of an idea put forth in earnest. Rather, it comes through as a construct the poet has found to her liking, already implicit in the sounds and sights themselves of Italy, "this place where all the pretty roots of words are."

The real test is getting the culture home, like yogurt kept warm in an immigrant's bodice during the long crossing. Agoos slips gracefully through Customs. Rhythms to the speech, logic to the television tower, farm scenes, town meetings, the haunting "Lunar Eclipse at a New England Funeral"—forms present from the start are now easier to perceive. The four cardinal points, the four seasons? Without a single baroque painter to personify them, haven't we known by instinct how vital, how useful, such notions are? Here is the way Agoos develops one of these motifs in her book:

> No one has unlocked
> the incidental farmhouse
> from its four views,

she writes in the first poem, "Living Here." And later, in a poem wonderfully evoking Weather as an old laborer in the fields:

> Where *is* beauty, except
> in the ground, like this idea
>
> of a crossroads in a field? Does continuity
> count for nothing? At winter's end
> the fields are wide open,
>
> and it would be easy for the weatherman,
> or me, ignoring the four
> seasons, to lie down in them.

Finally, these crossings and quarterings having become second nature, like the steps of a folk dance, she is given a startling glimpse: living quarters, herself centered there, rising from her lover's bed, snowlit and on the move:

> Covering myself,
> your four mirrors struck me: gazing at
> myself in a fine state, I saw, four times,
> a quick stirring sweep you, like a last
> dream, beneath the sheets . . .
>
> And I went, thinking:
> Hurry. Already the sea is wet and
> the waves unhesitating . . .

This moment of truth, too fleet to count as self-knowledge, holds nonetheless in a flash the figure of a young artist fully occupying a space until now impersonal or traditional. What would the insight augur in practice? Perhaps "The Search" gives a clue. Agoos dedicates it to her sister, from whom as a child she learned the Latin names of trees and shrubs. The poem reads like an elegy—if not for a person, then arguably for the sentimental pedant its author didn't grow up to be. It begins:

> Recalling terms you threw to me on walks,
> I asked for you among the trees . . .

and ends:

> Whom were you reassuring with Latin names?
> What love made you believe the earth was stirred
> to take you in? Though often enough I've caught
> your track in snow, stark, and cavernous as scars
> that last forever on the Fagus, even the Betulae,
> like cliques of graceful women, scorn you now,
> white with pity, graceful and paperthin.
> I cannot blame them, nor the blushing Acer
> who fades unmoved by your particular step.
> That bark is not your skin, and roots long sunk
> in moss do not drink rain for you, or carry
> your memory to be dug at like a scent.

The dryads of this passage cannot distract a reader from the point. Indeed they enforce it: things sooner or later shrug off the glamor of even their finest names, and ask to be clothed in fresh language. The sister's Latin no longer becomes the trees. It will be *her* sister—Julie Agoos—whose words may one day do that.

—James Merrill

Acknowledgments

Some of the poems in this book, often in slightly different versions, first appeared in the following publications:

Antaeus: "Porto Venere"
The Antioch Review: "Suicidio"
The Boston Monthly: "Portrait from Senlis"
Crazyhorse: "An Early Translation"
padan aram: "The Search"; "After Snowfall"; "Edge of the Schoolyard"
Partisan Review: "Lunar Eclipse at a New England Funeral"
Pequod: "At Ponte a Mensola"
Poetry Northwest: "American Patriotic"
Quarry West: "Living Here"
Quarterly West: "Preparing to Move"
Western Humanities Review: "Franklin"
The Yale Review: "Florence Interlude"

I am especially grateful for the generous support of my teacher, the late Robert Fitzgerald. My thanks go also to David St. John, James Richardson, Rita Manzini, and Jane Shore.

I

It will do me no good to own land.
Through space the universe grasps me
and swallows me up like a speck;
through thought I grasp it. —Pascal

Living Here

I caught the owner outdoors by himself—Frost

I. From this upper pasture
    the whole hill falls
    like an immense parcel
    wrapped in the same green paper
    I've seen stored in your house—that Cuban
    lime color. And knots,
    one after another,
    tie henhouse to saphouse to tractor
    and stubble the sloped fields.
    Down at the church, ribbons

    of foxglove, sweetpea, begonia.
    Bulls still lunge at a necklace
    of stones around the birch,
    carving primitive
    stick figures with their rough horns,
    your initials also
    visible, a black
    thickness in the throat,
    beneath which hers
    are penned into a heart.

    No one has unlocked
    the incidental farmhouse
    from its four views.
    Your grandfather's father might still
    point out the proud avalanche
    of orchard grass, and his rocky tillage
    on the listening hill, the haypatch
    that sags into the blue
    abdomen of Kearsarge.
    The dark road is still pebbled with acorns.

II. "We old-timers," you begin,
     "should learn how to read the paper."
     All week you've been haying in rain.
     We are running our hands over beans,
     peppers, sweet corn, sharing
     a beer at noon and trading
     news, allergies,
     tales of the quick fall
     and the hard winter. Below us,
     an oarsman is caning the water.

III. Wind, too, drops down,
     like hands upon your house—
     ardent, holding the cupolaed
     barn apart so that
     the weathervane, cocked
     at an anxious angle, seems ill
     with looking forever South.
     At an hour like this one, even
     the clouds are bound on a perilous
     journey above that spot.

IV. All throughout March,
     smoke rose from the corrugated
     tin roof of the saphouse.
     The field, like an outstretched palm,
     just cupping the unseeded garden,
     offered you up at nightfall. Tired,
     you might clean a rifle. And I,
     if I happened to be here, would head
     home, twisting my neck around
     until I could no longer see your house.

     One day you fell through the roof
     of the well. Lying in the foot
     of freezing water, seeing the sky
     reduced to a blue moon,
     the disaster of snow sweeping

the cool eye of the tunnel,
you made promises to your children;
you remembered your father and mother.
Climbing the cold wall,
you wondered who had moved the well.

I'm taking you south, you told her,
or thought you did—a whisper
that traveled the 200 yards,
like your slow footprints, toward the dry
light of the picture window—childish
in the frozen fabric of your jumpsuit:
These winters are too cold to make worthwhile.
I'm fine right where I am, she said,
come in; it's you that's cold. She thought
you were making a riddle, a romance.

But now, the skin on your hands is pale
and on your face, the pigment
entirely faded. And 500
feet down, a sign beside
the house comes clear: the new well
you've dug all summer, meant to carry
450 gallons of ice-cold,
daily water into
the lives of whoever you find
bold enough to succeed you here.

V. Each day nameless,
except for some term of weather.
Moonlight could not make
a sight braver than this one is:
from here watching the white
spire crowning the village,
the boast of the bridge as it crosses
over the railroad, ghostly,
the dandelions are filling up
the emptiest half-acres,

and blow across August. Only the cattle
treading the silver grade
of the pasture seem ever to speak
of the long sorrow of living here
and dying somewhere else.
Below us, the same boat
drifts on a duller plane
of water, almost like a flat
star, colder than the rest, unmarred
by any call, or fisherman, or fish.

VI.   I ask you has Cordelia softened.
      "Oh, she's against it; says she won't move.
      That's progress for you, I guess."
      Which is more important, land
      or marriage? "Someone should be living
      here," you answer. Weak-kneed, I can feel
      my breath drawn off like cream;
      you hitch your trousers up
      as if proposing to me:
      Could you care for this?

VII. When you brought her north from her home in Texas,
      you'd been away nine years.
      In the blossom you break off and give me,
      your 50 years together
      are all crying: fool!
      it was you who proved citrus could grow here!
      "She's rooted now." Are you comforting me
      for my own guilty longing? You shrug as only
      a farmer can; lemon
      spits on your pied knuckles.

      She's out this minute picking berries
      from the barbed wire fence along the power line.
      She's been gone too long; her shoulder
      isn't mended. "At our age
      our fathers had been dead 10 years."

I feel ashamed at my age
is the way you mean it. Yes,
I am telling myself. I feel
I have somehow come between you
simply by loving the place so well.

VIII.   Her green thumb has been
held up to this so often;
her paintings hang in all
the houses. And her flowers, married
to the field at the edge of the garden,
neat as her cropped head
or a heart in good order, are fortressed
like the sun whose swift decisions
send morning, afternoon,
and evening back where they came from.

IX.   "Better there for us than here," you're saying.
"Someone young should be living here."
Then you warn me it's not easy; I know
by now how idiosyncratic
the peach is, and the pear,
and the wood that lasts only year
to year—far less than the eye
takes in at first glance, or the wide feeling
the heart gives to the rib,
that glance, as the gentler heart gives in.

"Yes," I tell you, "I would
like to live beside the barn"
knowing the four winds
that courted you, quartering
every year since then,
so that no one besides you, coming
or gone from the hill, has known
the gift of living long
within its simple chamber,
this still lookout one climbs to.

X. But the day is struck with your going.
Clouds in the distance break
as if to move on, but do not;
the pink hills cross
and uncross themselves; the trees,
the boat all quiver red
as the sound of cymbals; everything
is rigged, stopped—like your old throat,
or sweet talk escaping from an older
man to a younger woman.

Portrait from Senlis

The first time that I saw her I was shy:
Madame Duranti in her rocking chair,
dusting her slippered feet along one square
of tiled floor. Then, looking up, she stared,
beckoning with a cigarette, gold-tipped,
and indicated where I ought to sit
without a word of welcome. Arch face lit,
she discoursed roughly, in a mannish way,
on furniture from Asia, rocks, how day-
light hit peculiarly the window bay.
"An invalid," she said, "should never wed.
Why bother with a husband, when instead
a doctor keeps you company in bed?"
And laughed and said, "It's crude, but so am I."

Madame received on Sundays, knowing I
was easy in her high-walled room and played
piano she might listen to. I stayed
for dinner on the nights she was afraid
to be alone, not out of charity
but gratified that she felt safe with me,
so fascinated by her dignity
I would have stayed a month, though she delighted
in declaring she abhorred the self-invited.
And when she said, "You *know* I'm second-sighted?"
I said, "*Tell me*—" but she laughed and said, "I lie."

She was never overbearing; still, with pride
she graciously received and from her bed
directed whiskey to be poured, and read
descriptions from a travel guide. She said,
"One must see everything, and when one's through,
one must *try* everything, then do
as much again. You see? I'm telling you

that God created man to travel and
you must decide—" Then, stretching out her hand—
"And be content to die if not a man
and not a minute has escaped your eye."

Franklin

On this day of the week,
hardly anyone rises
up over the slope that leads
from the trees' shadows back south to the highway.
Alone on the wide street the car rocks sideways.
An old woman rocks in a green swing;
her small feet hanging
neatly crossed
swing and disappear and swing
over a low barrow of impatiens.

Next day a single shutter has come sheer
from the second story.
Green water drips from a green gutter,
missing the newsboy, who is
used to the local weather. You notice this,
in passing, from the car;   and, more noteworthy:
the naked *I* in the IGA;
Boats To*I*Let (has that one been put here?);
Cold Beer*IES;*
a new hole—perhaps from a bullet—
muting the Town P pulation.
An older target, always a joke, stays pinned
to the door of the Fish & Game Club:
BACK ONE TUESDAY. GONE FISHING.

Past the storefronts full of yarn and hardware,
past three sagging restaurants, the last
of South Main Street, which drew the borders
of four settlements
into a well-knit town
and paper city.
The Central Street is hidden across the bridge,
laid out by halves, in brick and plateglass, granite,
wood, and wedged into the space carved by two rivers—
its crowded neighborhood

of dams and falls,
the ruined Needle Co. and woolen mills
gone in a glance.
Past prison, Pike's Lumbers, Soeurs de Ste. Croix (set back),
dust from the gutted road cuts blows up
shimmering, bad-tasting, red
on the car seat—not any cure for it but not
any cause for worry.
Nothing stops the heart. The town clock
is funny, rather than sad or annoying.

This old meeting ground is like that.
Oh, late in the year,
when the water in Webster Lake
hardly drifts,
the wet moss reappearing everywhere
recalls with a certain loveliness
some old farmer who gave in,
and for a while the local papers raise a thousand issues
all about Loss, and there's an acute
and lovely quiet.
A barn falls,
and a beech gripping a lightning cable,
and a cake, and a prize nest,
and a man from the Merrimack Valley outpost
along with a telephone pole.
The tale comes round again,
like strike, or flood,
to Mrs. Phillip Call—scalped
by Indians, her family kidnapped
in the years of early purpose.
Someone's male cat returns
only to return small bodies
to a neighbor's doormat.
There is a long argument
over chickens, about coydogs.

But most afternoons,
hunters pull off their red jackets,
their wives pull on jackets, and from

some summer body's lakeside lawn
they might watch somebody's white canoe appear
in the round eye at the flag end
of a tall steel sculpture fixed in the ground before them;
then, sail through the eye
as if it were a hoop
actually suspended half in air,
half in water: first the bow and then the whole boat
emerging into open water towards them,
without any visible movement
or break in the lens.

This sight is a favorite illusion among the townfolk,
who view the town as somehow powerful,
just as a diver from Franklin, plunging into
the town pool, might say
that his displacement as he shoots
down into water
is not much different
from what the water feels.

Making History

Here we sit, a model audience,
inviolable as the Ordinance,
upright, without a cause, nor sigh, nor strife:
a row of wives. Though I am not a wife,
but yes, a woman, I, too, have memorized
each number on each folding seat, the size
and site of each prized lot and every tree
whose fate we're gathered now to oversee.
I am not grim-faced, stump-jawed, country, old
enough to dose myself—unless I'm told—
with apple-jack. But I am curious enough
to linger until peace is made a part of
our assembly's fragile bond. For I insist
I belong to this race of knitters—true, not least
because their future protects mine; you see,
I know their needle war intimately
having always worn the season's wool
against the winter's thrust and summer's pull.
The wife before me has a trembling back.
I recognize the mood, the rising stack
of stitches cast, the seasoned stitch dismounted
by the one behind me (one foot having counted
purls as proudly as a diver might
show off his catch) now disposing of the right
or left sleeve—of a length I must assume
is sleeve enough for someone in the room.
For our men are marrow; hangers; backs:
mere form ingrained in us, like the tracks
they leave behind them—gone without a word
of praise or thanks; and covered or uncovered
matters less to us, in time, knowing
we've gained a certain power by their going,
simply by what we do, take comfort from—
like shuttles turning on the sturdy loom
their independence to the common good. To women then!
in false assembly in a room of men

whose young Contender has yet to discover
subtlety enough, or wile, to win them over.
Let him look to our ranks, emulate
our bull-willed faces if he'd alter fate
by challenging the Variance, and laws
most firmly written. Let him prove his cause
to us, as nature does—the minds of men
are often closed; and then he might begin
to build here, with us crafting history
for violent seasons and posterity.

Edge of the Schoolyard

Quitting the class in hordes, the double doors
—their painted faces cracked, and square edges
chewed into splintery roundness—trembled
and swung back into the empty room;
hung uncertain and forlorn within
that quiet disarrangement; waited perhaps.

There was a hive outside the library window.
The quietest, at times, might be allowed
out, on certain afternoons, to hear
the wasps called back to honey.
                                        Bells at midday
never seemed so sweet to us as that.

There was a willow and a pond, this
side of the graveyard, where I stripped the most
exhausted branches when they arced and fell
in coils, and played the Greek there: bound
both feet and ankles; fashioned thick laurel wreaths
out of the crippled cord. There was a fence
so tangled in the overhang it seemed
to spring from it—link by link, as roots,
the green vinelike metal kept us in;
the barbed rim with its peculiar teeth
ground in warning. So we watched the peaceful
burials, heard the salute of guns,
like felons barred from sympathy, or even
wonder, after many years.
                                        Moody,
I learned there to break with friends again
and again, or else to lose more confidently,
for the willow's sake and tender beauty.

Then it appeared to us that flight was flight
no matter where one went, though silence ruled
at recess as they dug the pits and carried
flags and draped the tombstones sweetly for
the love of the dead returning; still in quick
formation
                as if all of them, the diggers,
mourners, veterans were one,   for each
understood retreat: no one reproached
our keen arrival . . .

                        Winters, skating skateless
on the ragged ice beneath the great
tree's canopy—the fragile latticework
of leafless limbs now greying, soft as string—

I often saw the buried pocket money:
copper coins of fall leaves, some crescent-
shaped, like fearing eyes, young moons gleaming
blankly from the blank encasing sky
like mine. Or were they mine
                            reflected there?

The Sitting

They said the temperature would drop. And I
am being paid, after all, for this
stillness: like the goodest of good girls
as lovely as I can be, endlessly
happy; captured by their happiness
—that slow, suspended scraping as they temper
me on glass, mingle the dusk-olive
of my sharp-boned cheek with warmer pinks,
spreading the fever gently. How deftly they
transpose the animated palette! How
that pinched white canvas soon becomes me!
They, looking like fishwives with their aprons,
knives, and stands—drily appraising, filleting—
must weight the scales at times. Yet it appears
I'm in good hands. They know my hem is straight,
and all my wild hair is set in oils
and glows with a distinctly bold style.

I must have grown from this, must be some other
woman, propped and eager for attention,
such abandon greets me in those eyes
modeled on mine. Is that how they first
saw me, like a doll in need only
of dyes and stitching? Is that why they stroke
me busily, as if I might grow faint
on canvas, freeze to death and only half-dressed?

Am I worthy? Nothing in the room
to look at besides me, nothing to care for;
all their motion putting me to sleep.
And yet they say that I sit well. Will I
come back, they ask (but surely as if they
regret the hourly change as I do). Well,
perhaps. I like it here. I feel deserted
being watched by these five pairs of eyes
reflecting peace I feel nowhere inside.

Is this what I'm good at? Vain, surely,
but silent glory?
            Soon, they bring me tea
as black as oil slick and paint the steam
more quickly than it rises . . . how could
I once have hoped to be as everlasting
as that graceful rendering of heat?

Grandmother Thinking

The train comes into the station like sluggish water,
rocking in its bay, flat with dust,
as we stand watching from the same exotic
distance water raises between itself and us:

The train is a mirage, a long moment
of uncertainty—like the deer
so often startled in the dusk, their fear
palpable to us who also fear life slipping past

on the breeze of each departure and arrival,
though sometimes, from our tidepools, waiting, it seems
that we've accumulated here only by
the merest chance, that we are all escaping love—

then love is raised up in us, who have
nothing to fear by now, no particular wants.

Lunar Eclipse at a New England Funeral

At the funeral, we sing a hymn
she sang for us so often that our voices
in the cold church are cloudy, and tentative:
concentrating so hard on death,
we can almost hear her as the organ softens.
Then in the silence after the last prayer,

we whisper our way past the coffin leaving flowers
as if we could obscure that heavenly image.
We sigh the long way to the graveyard through tall grass;
along the ground, our stilt shadow bodies
slide off into the blackberry bushes. We can hear
the toads and crickets passing over them,

the crushed sound of the grass, and the crumpled lilacs
falling into a mass of shadow lilacs
already lying there. Several low notes
sound from an owl, and each grows shorter.
From the pasture above the graveyard, the coydogs' howls
collect like a fabulous blanket over us:

the moon, the sort of federal color she most
admired, has a creeping softness that increases
each quarter hour. And suddenly the air
is so sensitive! We smell the scent
of lilacs on her table, hear her grace,
high and ardent, see ourselves, grouped

like a nimbus in the lampglow by the old piano:
Fight the Good Fight, she trills, while the gentle
shadows pressed against the parlor windows
soon overlay the house; the slow,
profound voice of the honorable
reverend, murmuring, *O, Lord, protect,*

and rolling over the swelled ground toward us,
slips into the shadow of our crescent
like the indirect moonlight now
disappearing in earnest under the rolling
shadow of this blank planet. And there are strange
pictures in all he says, until we wonder

where the dead go, who are the dead?
Her dog lies down beside the granite tombstone,
a voice calls: *hush, Gulley, hush* . . .
Her long name glowing last
is draped in a ribbon of darkness like a statue,
and we are divided from her forever now.

But how much greater she seems to us since
we have seen just how the earth makes its full
exchanges; and how death is not, not really
like this place, but public, historical,
in it each moment of the cycle
—month, day, hour, slow minute

and slower second—completely torn apart;
most of all, that it has already happened to her,
leaving us here. Another hour will bare
one darkened half of this family graveyard,
and though the reverend, murmuring again
Lord, save her!, seems to us half savior, half devil,

for now it is easy to wait: standing on solid
ground, shadowless, we see images
of fire, whole cities dotting the darkness.

Arrival

As if we had just woken later than usual,
finding only the dim light of afternoon,
and of the station lights wastefully burning
on the street that could be any other
that leads us to a small bed and breakfast
facing the water, like an old arena
outlined by green benches: a stillness, for a while
staring at the brown edges of lampposts supported
by concrete blocks in the water, catching a scent
of something we remember but cannot name.

I say we will go looking for it later
in accents that have not improved with time,
and sit trying to locate the image that brought us here
—whose past it was we wanted to enter—
when you say: anyhow, it's beautiful enough.
And I look at the boats tethered to their gold
patches of sea, and at the gold embellishment
of names along the sterns and starboard bows,
and realize that half the world is this familiar.
Then in the level water stretching between the boats,
vaguely distorting our arrival, how many
serene depths there would be;   and my desire
to stay here and claim it as a homecoming
by this time has become so elaborate,
though it started from nothing, that I do not answer.

Terzo Piano

You lucky man among all the armor!
Your window, your five-hour roost, looks out
on a courtyard, the careful fulfillment of angles
upheld by a tiered arrangement of loggia
and walls, this perfectly empty house
supporting you on your third story. Hermit
you are, and parent, having guarded
forever the small transits of scholars
through the Bargello, their shadows like columns
fallen into a wheel from every
half-lit hall and gallery: Time
turned for now into the shadows of bronze
bells in the court, soundless, still rational,
laying down their permanent truth.

Below you, Cellini's messenger
is rising on soft wings, his fingers
long and sun-gilt, straining forward
—like Victory breaking chains—toward heaven.
Climbing the stairs a herd of quiet
tourists gains dimension on the second *piano,*
then drawn by Giambologna's taller
Mercury, drifts between the loggia arches,
separate as mountains
though so far off—
yet you see in that ascension
all things losing their density;
from here you have seen so much desire
move toward you, as if the world
were a chain of your own making.

Your timid elbow moves as if
there were a man inside your armor!
The hinge of your bent arm leaves
a shining spot of oil against your ribs.
And I, finding a space at the ledge beside you,

am wary as you are—remembering
how Florence conquered Pisa and her flesh grew stony—
when, from an opposite cell
on the *terzo piano,* a man calls out to you,
and his wife, searching deep in her guidebook
(trying to place us because she loves him
more than ever now), says
something loud and wise and foolish:
Oh my darling, look: how life
imitates art in the young afternoon.

An Early Translation

Dinda was eighty,
so thoroughly admired
she could not age any more.
And under the shade tree
where I first inquired
whether she would come indoors
(where Norma had made tea
and a brief, strong fire),
she sat plaiting a bunch of wildflowers
with a straight wire:
per seccare, she assured me,
and that needed no translating.

There was no fire
in her house, nor talk for warmth,
only the warm henhouse where her hens
laid hourly, or once, so many white
eggs that she was forced into making
several journeys as she carried them
from her house to ours.

Black frock, black socks, black boots,
her entire body by then
a black storm, a cloud
settled in on the stoop and waiting
for someone to let her in or to deny her,
lifting the poor nest of reeds when I answered,
like a hornet she gave me a look
of such pure desire
that I took the basket from her fading hands
(my own stung pink against her black attire)
and placed it beside the basket of fruit
seeing the apples and oranges offer their warmth to her,
like gravy coloring the plates
at noon left empty
to dry on the sideboard.

By now it was evening again. Nothing chattered.
Her two teeth disappeared like pilings
in a purse of water, as I tried holding forth
on my own to her, in Italian:
how I came to be
in that room, by that fire.
Without any music to lend
a form to my story, still she paid me
a complement of gestures,
wild, tender, knifesharp—
bold as the furniture repeating, spatially,
all that I uttered; or the fire itself
half mortal, also explaining, while the shadows of her black arms,
in a holding pattern for hours, draping the words
in sense, drew the room in closer,
whole as a hammock.

I never understood then why her
manner grew suddenly formal, stiff,
but outside, I knew, the weighty
anemones had closed,
grown tired under the deft wind
that tore each evening through the foreign
countryside so like a great lady's garden.
And knew the sun,
with its briarlike reflections,
would warm and open them in the morning:
how fadeless
the flowers would be then, flaring like fire,
trimmed into a far more stately posture.

Porto Venere

A battle has risen:
under the spreading
armory of clouds,
there is a tumult
of footfall down
the terraced hillside,
and hands, invisible
in the brush,
grasping and letting go,
start up a shimmer
of motion like a petticoat's
and small landslides
of stone start
in the yellow grass.
We hear the rustle,
the bobbing upwards
of branches—sounds
of camouflage so much
like the recovery
of a New England orchard
all spring and summer.

Wind knocks
grapes from the trellis.
There is a volley
of breeze and raindrop.
In the hills
the olive leaves
turn up their silver
sides, just as
the sea keeps turning
over, a dark
finger's width
of light there
below us. And all
along the wharves the litter

of *gelati* and *lire*
skitters forward
into the harbor,
and the siren of air
and cats wailing
tears at the clouds,
revealing an instant
of shuddering seacraft,
the Gothic campanile,
while we too
concealed in the sun's
struggle lean back
in our chairs,
hearing the wind
on the cobblestone,
in the street's fatal
undercurrent:
the old man's cough,
the shutters being closed,
every taut
clothesline humming.
Then even the scent
of figs   finds its way
in the sudden rain
to desert us.

We admire the narrow
houses that blush
in each quick blade
of sunlight: how
they crowd against the hillside
pale orange
and grey   and pink
and straight black lines,
like delicate drawings
on fieldmaps;   and how
they are unlike
the pale pink calamari
losing their color
in the storm's ambush.

And admire the squid
we could not finish:
half liquid, half solid,
filling the white
dish—a complement
of land and water;
and its blackness
rising no higher
than the white rim:
that pure design
and self-containment
of two colors,
like the pure black eye
of a white summer
flower, in no danger
of losing its foreignness.

An Afternoon's Activity

for Peter and David Michaelis

All night the train, no sleep, the deaf conductor
shouting to us at Tarantella.
We left there, and came here, sleepwalkers.

> *In dreams, each plane*
> *rising and roaring*
> *or in a descent*
> *too steep to dare the land*
> *heads for the ocean.*
> *I am a frozen passenger,*
> *feeling a steady heat*
> *beneath my ribs.*

Above the door there are three red stars.
"Caveat Emptor," Diana says, alert,
"o sono queste le porte del Paradiso?
If not, we could do ourselves a lot of harm."

> *Awake, I cannot*
> *reconstruct*
> *what sea it was,*
> *what land the flight*
> *had come from; why*
> *I feel hope and fear.*

Still we go in through this *porta principale,*
passing our bags to the solemn *portiere*
("chi porta un fiore all'occhiello, vedi?")
and whose gait (*portamento*), with its
slow preamble, makes us laugh some more.

> *Never mind, never mind.*
> *Dio, ho fame.*

Later we find it's just a guidebook rating
meaning: the best (*il migliore*) to indicate

that we should stay and eat. And in the vaulted
cellar, where the fat cook keeps
a mythic rule (forbidding all talk except
on the subject of food), the young *camerieri*
strut table to table, *e ci domandano*
cosa possono portare. "Che inferno,"
Diana says, removing her red shawl.

> *Trees flare. Outside*
> *my son's window*
> *planes of the upright*
> *oak tree romance*
> *the passive pine.*
> *And from the maple*
> *three red leaves*
> *fall and scatter.*
> *Their shadows blush*
> *on his young cheek*
> *as he bends to write me,*
> *while on the table,*
> *everything I own*
> *makes claims on him:*
> *the flask of yellow*
> *oil bellied out*
> *beside the orchid-full;*
> *the pumpkin china plates;*
> *pitcher and winestems*
> *ribboned round*
> *with purple overflows;*
> *dunes of linen!*

Then in the afternoon, I leave her nested
in blankets in the small bed beside
the *portafinestra* and the *portacatino.*
"I think I've found my port of call," she says,
flipping through the pages of her thick
vocabolario; and I take this as a great
sign of health, and tell her so. "You can think
what you like, so long as it brings me luck," she answers,
"but maybe you should get it down in writing.

At least we can give the postman something to do." *Tua*
madre si sente di essere in porto,
the postcard I will write next says.

> *O let the sudden*
> *quilting of the leaves*
> *be respite to him!*

But going out of the Porta Rosa, doors
that I do not remember opening beget
more doors—just as those wooden child-women
open and reveal more children: through the lens
of anterooms, barren of all but a stray *portaombrelli,*
from each slow arch, the hazy sinopia
of mother and child with flowers holds me in its gaze,
eyes collapsed as if the world were nothing to them
now that they no longer have the power to move.

> *By my son's flushed*
> *cheek, the colorless*
> *window is discreet*
> *as midafternoon.*
> *Light enters*
> *as fairies are said to,*
> *unafraid to sink*
> *between disorders;*
> *in the green half-bottles*
> *turning the tension lines*
> *like wine to acid.*
> *I wake up worried,*
> *feeling selfish.*

Nothing moves at two in the piazza:
white statues bronze under the dry
spirals of *sole, fontana.* Even the postcard
flat on the green bench could be from you
or for you, could be a plaque to someone: permanent.
Without tea or passersby, what
I see are only incremental changes:
cars where no cars were; a cloud of bicyclists

backpedalling by the curb, who race for distance,
and whose loud and unexpected voices
journey much as the eye does, as free
at times within the empty space the body fills.
Carried here without intention, or any real meaning,
they are at once foreign and heartbreaking.

"Sì, può portarci molto danno, la vita,"
like this strange genealogy of hours
in which already she has formed a middleground,
a place where all the pretty roots of words are,
between that small room with its empty
portafiori (*flower stand*) and this unused daylight
I have walked into without her.
The sun in my lap as I try writing this postcard
is an exclamation mark (punto),
an emphasis of what the sun was.

> *O, figlio,*
> *I am not*
> *beautiful, here,*
> *portando gli occhiali*
> *hanging on*
> *my swelled bosom,*
> Herald International
> *spilled across*
> *my knees, portacappelli,*
> *portacarte,*
> *portacipria,*
> *portafogli,*
> *portacenere,*
> *portafrutta,*
> *everything still*
> *strewn everywhere*
> *around me. O,*
> *che letto di rose!*
> *Ma spero che stia*
> *in ogni caso*
> *alle porte*
> *quando arrivano*
> *queste lettere,*
> *quando arriverò,*
> *e quando vado via.*

Florence Interlude

At noon, on the stair's
elbow, the light falls,
and soon each pair
of pensioners comes down, the walls

darkening with their shadows.
At a square window, at a square table,
the sun allows
that they are capable.

Here is a blonde
English girl, a German couple
getting on
in years, a supple

man always reading
a red book,
a tired nanny feeding
her own child: Look,

she says, as the spoon stirs
the white foam,
don't you want it? Look! as her hand shutters
the tiny spoon, like the handsome

man now keeping the glare from his pages,
how the statue's broken eyes assume
a blinding look—then grow ageless
and opaque across the room.

Isn't it terrifying
how a shadow visits?
They are verifying
the light, its

historicity,
this hour that gives
a past to the city,
what of their own lives?

wondering now, as the sun eavesdrops
over their private stay here:
what have they given up?
What if the cost grows dearer?

Here is a view,
here is a postcard,
a pen, a bright new
stamp, a glance toward the window, a glance inward.

But look how the statue
even now detaches
self from the marble self and from those few
elegant scratches.

Portinaio

Here is a room to come to,
one with chairs enough;
here are books to choose from
just as the stingy light does,
leaving its impress on each wall,
while the stone brute lies guarding us,
and this old portinaio
(far more capable
of movement than we are)
comes setting the floor astir

with something closer to grandeur
than impatience: pulling the broom,
a square bit of tapestry
drags into the room beneath it,
just like a hooked fish
half rising out of flystruck
water: how at home he is,
bending backward like an angler,
moving through the room
back first, his flexed thighs

and puffed-out ribs, blue-covered,
mirroring the sky—a perfect
Eastern reverence
now carrying him all around
the twelve chairs we're sitting in,
that girdle the lustrous table,
making the scene more metaphorical
to us; to him, more blessed—
for when I say *buon giorno,*
he does not turn—

his voice trembles—then he bows
as if the river shielded him. Ah,
for a man like that, who assumes
some majesty within me
without demanding it!
And I call to him again
and see the hot blush
start beneath his collar,
too late how his body, spine-arced,
his vision now altered, had been

preparing him to turn
from the western window, where
he stands straight at last,
gazing out—having left
a wide circumference,
a dull planet circled
on the wood stretching between us,
as if the sun had been
where he has been, not
yet heating the place I come from.

High on the mantel, a crowned
Madonna is as faithless
to the forms the world
holds out to us, and reaches
her hand around her child
into handpainted
scenes of Eden troubling
that high south wall. What wouldn't
she exchange, gladly,
for a single taste

of that cadmium yellow apple?
And Maddalena, what
type is she, beside
that other Mary covered
in dust he cannot reach?
Or, bearing her own child,
can she have quelled that rumor,

this repeated history?
Che bella giornata comes
to me on a rare lightwave,

and I am at home now.
But where is the third mother,
is that what his soft broom is asking?

Suicidio

Non domandarci la formula che mondi possa aprirti,
sì qualche storta sillaba e secca come un ramo.
Codesto solo oggi possiamo dirti,
ciò che non *siamo, ciò che* non *vogliamo.*

—Montale

I come on this six months after
hearing a similar story It's March,
a time for writing about rivers.
I am heading to the Borgo Ognissanti,
to the Hotel Albion, where each
American-named child of the family
Balderini is sure to be looking
after something, my joy or sorrow.

This is how they separate
themselves from any lingering surprise
since the father died by falling from
the second floor, when a weak riser
gave out in the staircase, and they became
like several pigeonholes recessed
side by side—still enclosing
all the year-old correspondence
that descended here—a poste
restante, an oak grille, an iron
weir in the newly tiled lobby.

And this is how I separate
myself from all the watermarks
that rise like a stairway from the Arno,
and from the soot-covered plaques that bear
the darker legend of November Fourth:
how, since nothing *is* unified,
I give up my share in that cold anniversary.

What makes me suspect the water now
is that careless surface heading nowhere,
and the pinched look of the bridges reaching
far down, for once far past
their superficial shadows; and

the colorlessness of the flood tide;
the leaves that keep as dry as autumn
swirling down to form another
sort of independent body
floating there.

        So that I stand for a moment
wondering whether there are five
bridges more after all, or whether
one bridge keeps on repeating
five echoes in the slow miles
backing off toward the Apennines,
when I see a young geometrist
I know a little, whose gesture of alarm
as he stands by the Ponte alla Carraia
alarms me; and watching him pack up his canvas
and notebooks, hurrying off without once turning,
I recall how he once pronounced
a simple theory to a crowd of us
in the Blue Grotto at Fiesole:
non si può mai frenare
la volontà—one can never
contain the will, or the shape, of a thing.

And suddenly that bridge spanning
the pulpits of the Carmine
and Santa Maria Novella seems
no more than a pale cross-section of
the bodies of Massaccio and Uccello.
And the shouts of the blue-smocked fishermen,
and the whispers of women, and all of the effortless
chatter of children cannot keep
the brown leaves from falling face
down; nothing can move me beyond
the curve of the river, for the leaves
eye themselves like brittle soldiers
who will never be buried, and nothing will
dispel this image from Montale,
nor tarnish the water's clarity.

No one knows yet just what
we are watching. Nor whether the water contains
us or we contain the water,
yet it seems this is the will
of that older death, when, under the thick
diagonal of clouds that braces
the roofs and gives the city to the other Arno,
another crowd stood here on the Lungarno
watching a man throw himself
like honor on the current and
the delicate pattern of rings spread out,
subsiding delicately, trapped
between bridges.

        We know only that
the half-completed bridges
mimic us in their eral mood;
and know their suicidal impulses:
how each diminishing
arch escapes the city, seeming
a part of ourselves, and should have pleased us
were we only artists watching.

But for the one surviving,
North exists only in
a hard vertical, South:
where the father fell. Just as
the yellow leaves Montale troubled
are indeed lifeless if
they are not heroes; or as my eyes,
deep in the water, soon discover
remnants of the bombs once parceled
out to Florence: of that odd,
single life still afloat,
just like this single story spelling out
the moment only in relation
to my drawing close enough
to stand and see the body sink
down, and know it did not have to.

Then my eyes steady on mountains
in both directions; I cannot
think in any language
what these sights mean for now,
though I hear the river speaking to itself.

Quattro Stagioni

There's an ocean of turf today,
and the weatherman sits on the stoop
in the rain-cloud shadow of the doorframe,

and I come a great distance towards him
over the flat field,
seeing the four seasons

crossing with me—the field
a broad grid of flavors, elemental
bridges and ditches of seed

and survival. It's nearly summer.
The air is thick and loud
with a new air of voices, like children

pestering him: *Cosa*
hai fatto ieri, babbo?
Cosa fai oggi? Dove,

dove vai dopo, e poi?
He won't predict. His back aches;
age troubles him as it might a father

pacing that first afternoon,
when everything seems much closer
to him: all the unenlightened

space he had plowed into
at his winter labor,
that now climbs directly to the olive groves.

How is one to be alone
knowing one is not leaving
something? Could he really

be asking a question like this,
or (all the seasons tied
together intimately),

noticing, hearing myself
making tracks on the private ground,
have I simply imagined

that life is like this process
of the weather, or the patient
trudge of the painter, for whom

sight and sound are thinned
sometimes to nothing; who knows perfectly
well what supports him, but continues

to paint out of memory, giving
a dash of his own, when he's in
the mood, to the general background?

What does appearance mean then?
Where *is* beauty, except
in the ground, like this idea

of a crossroads in a field? Does continuity
count for nothing? At winter's end
the fields are wide open,

and it would be easy for the weatherman,
or me, ignoring the four
seasons, to lie down in them.

Above the Land

Hour of figs. The battleground of grass
is pink with them. And pierced by age, a few
unripened green ones falling. Weary too,
the violet sun silvers the olive trees.

Look, my brother says from another country,
Look at this petrified thing!   and I scream as he tosses
the hollow weight of a peach, and petrifies me.
Quick, the screen door on the white house beyond us bangs,
jolting the steeple and the Grange Hall, unsettling the lake,
as if I had summoned <u>that</u> sound out of myself
and set it in a wavelike motion through the landscape;
and then our neighbors would come out, listing and graceful,
come out to us as if from a long way.

There's a saying: it's a long day if you're waiting—well,
we hated to wait for that long chastening journey
across the lawn. Less tender every season,
how could I shout: *He's throwing peaches Mr. Mrs. Graves!*
and hope for their merciful judgment? Nor could we break
the silence that foretold a punishment
fear always made seem half-imagined;
although it never was comfort to know such belonging,
I cannot remember their old faces differently.

But here, instead of peaches there are figs.
Now in the pink contagion of the foggy season
only shape is recognizable,
time still working out its many lengths.
So I'll think of Cordelia pruning the flaccid peonies into July
to give as presents. Her husband atop his tractor
lean as a piece of equipment. Fond, how he'd say,
nodding his uncreased brow toward her great slow body:
You know a place and you get to love it.
These damn Yanks will pick up anything.

At Ponte a Mensola

I

Cows come here, and sheep, to drink
in the pumpkin shade of the monastery.
Waiting for spring, the fields are flat
and wounded. Punishing this season,
winter saw blades whirr each noon,
felling trees. Nobody knows
this place —*Ponte? What's the river there,
and what do they do for a living, drink coffee?
Sleep in the shade?*   If I knew, I might stay.

A stone plaque on the stone wall
of the Via Vincigliata lists
artists whose inspiration once added
a solemn, foreign appeal to the stillness.
Shelley lived on the Via D'Annunzio.
The people will recite you names
you'll recognize in accents you'll hardly follow;
and though the mangy riverbed
is nearly empty, some afternoons,
their cars lined up for cleaning on the banks,
hearing their songs from town
you'll imagine women singing
tunes taught them by nuns to scrub by,
hard-won water pouring over skin
as veined as fields, the suds deflating
in the reeds, like clouds. The monks
refer to it—this clarity
of winter sound—if you should ever catch them
dozing outside after a meal.
They are proud of the picturesque.
They will invite you, also, to sit down,
to imagine *their* gift:
the sacred life of the duecento
frescoes and the fine ceramic
bowls they bow to, eating in twelves.

All this makes worth remembering
the name: *Ponte a Mensola,*
although the bridge does not stem a tide
nor lead anywhere except between hills.

II

So much sensation is unknown.
On the banks of that river that parts the city
of Florence, should you straddle the wall,
your pink legs will glow in twilight,
hair fan up against the iron lampposts;
and the frank jaws of the bridges will be tranquil
—no couple nor autobus sways from its business,
gingerly framed in the open mouths—
the city on the water's surface
patient, economic as a painting
though the crowds press and call from the bridges.
Throughout the season of cold rain,
it will have been worth something to have
connected that life to your own existence:

that grey gallery is a horseshoe;
that dome is not Brunelleschi's, but
the bell that rang at Medici weddings;
that library reproved the whispers
of Leonardo—as if to live
in a foreign country, after all
(like the painted terra cotta tablets
climbing the walls of the similar buildings),
one must only learn to lie quite still
and without thinking, for hours so.

III

So much is invisible in this season.
Here, the women glide and stamp
between rows of greenness that sprout so,
I'd swear I'd taken the wrong turning.
I see their sacks get big. At this
distance, I can only imagine that their arms
have moved, they draw their kitchen knives
so deftly, sideways, through roots. At times
thinking *I don't envy these women,* then
I reprove myself by recalling my own
lack of grace among corn and blackberries—
No beauty is reflected here or there.
Just several men propped against trees
like scarecrows; like the painters who wade the unsteady
stream in spring, their legs are also missing,
somewhere received by the vertical field
of green trees. Now watching them whittle,
I'll think of that unclaimed sound of voices
that circles above the land: one cannot
enter the perspective without losing sight of it.
One loves what one is reminded of loving.

III

After Snowfall

I heard the last voices drift apart;
up stairs, through doors, calling out they put
themselves to rest. Bells stilled, or glass
breaking: how startled sound departs upon
the hour, sleep soon blanketing the choral
murmuring of sheets.
                  I heard the still
life breathing as a smile spreads
at dark between dark eyes; the memory
of conversation gleaming as the clock
does. It seemed, at one, we'd watched the snow
so long without speaking, there could be no other
speechlessness. But this was it: your house
sleeping. Somewhere in the dusky hall,
dreams stirred like cold breath mingling.

After snow, waking is never easy.
This bright morning turning towards the light
that bent the blinds in ribbons, carried smoothly
to my side as if a wave, hesitating,
moved me, I saw your body blazing
warm beside me; saw your winter skin
grow amber-red, and sun breaking over
it; and rose and marveled at your arms
thrust back behind your quiet head. A strong
arc of certainty rose with me: your
bare breast full of light: I wished you knew
that beauty
              and the window full of white
trees as breathtaking, sketched above the rippled,
white-rimmed sea; half-lit; still; and only
half waking. You know the rising light
outside on days like this: how it is pink,
briefly. And your purple slippers, too,
were pink; the blue sheets, untried and cool
at night now nearly green.

                              I became
an object, imitating: pulled the covers
up as though I might protect the soft
well of heat left by my own body
in that beam. Covering myself,
your four mirrors struck me: gazing at
myself in a fine state, I saw, four times,
a quick stirring sweep you, like a last
dream, beneath the sheets. Then the sea
breeze moved in and lightly joined your breathing.

In my own house, walking silently
on waking, as if someone might come walking
with me, I remeet each room. Now
taking leave of you, the same sense
enfolds me: I can't help myself, but take
a last look: everywhere the day
is broadly broken and the sun streaming;
morning hits the ceilings and the bright floors;
the high seats, the clear glass tables, and
the Delft plates that serve as ashtrays are
a painting: life well worth waiting for,
before leaving.
                    And I went, thinking:
Hurry. Already the sea is wet and
the waves unhesitating. Snow falling
from the roof reminded me: the house
was full again, and ready, and its voice
spoke: Hurry—sounds of your making.

February

In the house, without our mother in it,
spaces fill with meaning, as on those afternoons
spent waiting for the snow to fall: It's cold
for hours; breath is something new; then snow
follows like the least painful part of you.
My brothers plan a snowman for tomorrow,
and later, standing at my bedroom window,
show me, as she might have, how the lamp's a halo
throwing near-daylight on the steps up to the house.
Thinking, perhaps, that she'll forgive us now,
I vow never to forget this love I feel.
We still believe that empty space resolves itself
—like the unrenouncing fullness of the view,
for reasons inarticulate, but true.

American Patriotic

I look out the window onto new pavement.
In the sky, a fire is spreading. Peace,
you say, or Mahler says from somewhere nearby.

It's twilight by the television tower,
a band of dusk, a code of tiny lights
—green stars above a dark territory:

in the window, the grey shadows of birds
flicker past, no more real to us
than that shadow earth, a ceremony

that appears and disappears. We watch
our own images walk out onto
a road that neither settles nor rises:

the sunset growing blue and red and white,
blue uppermost, blue virginal. How can we fight
for them, knowing *we do not fight for the real*

but for shadows we make, and below us, the town sparkles
as if it were filled with heroes, lying
under this blood red flag, that black field?

The Search

for my sister

Recalling terms you threw to me on walks,
I asked for you among the trees, despairing
still, and jealous of true reverence;
like you I whispered, though without your pride,
fearing the brittle verdict of the leaves
but there was nothing. No limb spoke of you.
What changes since you forced the lesson out?
For everywhere the view remains, and true
in all essential indications: buds,
leaves, twigs, and everything in shade.
Do acorns fall with greater sense than sound?
Nothing falls quite the same way, you once said,
that powdery bursting, dull, yet quick as hail—
how did it go? Or, once beside a shrub,
spreading your wisdom like that gorgeous flower:
"Kalmia," you said; as one might dare
release a blind I took the word, a place
of trespass yielding—"Kalmia" repeated,
mispronounced. You frowned, and ever since
that bush has been the laurel, uninspired.

All process cures. I ought to recognize
your street, your door at least. I see you making
bold commitments to its mystery
so clearly, stretching your head back beneath
the brow of the Platani. Yet I fail,
remembering your joy, to feel the reason.
Whom were you reassuring with Latin names?
What love made you believe the earth was stirred
to take you in? Though often enough I've caught
your track in snow, stark, and cavernous as scars
that last forever on the Fagus, even the Betulae,
like cliques of graceful women, scorn you now,
white with pity, graceful and paperthin.

I cannot blame them, nor the blushing Acer
who fades unmoved by your particular step.
That bark is not your skin, and roots long sunk
in moss do not drink rain for you, or carry
your memory to be dug at like a scent.

Painting the Railing

All afternoon, like a mixture of snow and rain,
the old paint falls from the wooden railing.
And the hot wind, lifting the shower of flakes,
carries them over the porch; the lawn is scaling.

My arm is a plow, or a circling airplane.
I am giving a grain to something soft and fraying.
Powered by the faint wind as the knife scrapes,
I kneel along the porch like someone praying.

The white past of the porch ages the lawn.
I see the world this way, the world through slats:
a bird far off is like a chip of paint;
the elements seem indiscriminate.

And yet, the wind is not connected to the paint:
this chain of sight and sound is my own folly.
Some colors grip the wooden rail more fiercely;
grey is a color far from melancholy.

Is this how sacrifice becomes a hobby?
A kind of gentle failing in things handmade?
Or does desire simply tend to imitate
the art of the sun on the lawn: now coupled, now faded?

The project aches with so much swift revising
though on the ground the ants, still concentrating,
are linked like a detail of paint, or like the railing
whose smooth future I go on contemplating.

The Good Neighbor

[The speaker addresses an ivory figurine.]

You look like an old professor of mine.
And as with him, I cannot now sort out
awe from affection, a feeling of safety from worry.
He knew more. He, with his bad heart,
gave out a sort of principle of heart,
found humor in the awful softening
that came with each attack on it, in each
it made (loving some particular
of learning) on oversized heroes bearing arms,
on folio fragments come into full being,
on all absurdist theatre—even
on the Chinese doctoral candidate
who fled from the foot of his armchair once when he'd placed
her well-made essay, page by page, onto
the floor beside her, reading it as they
drank tea. Later, he compared it to the kenning:
her soft-footed fury at the unmeant dishonor, the insult
limited and circumscribed by language,
yet all with the still precision of a watchspring:
the incompleteness of it and the timing.

Curious, the metaphor of action
turning us all to skeptics or professors,
he was fond of saying.
                         You look like him,
luck journeyman, given to me to serve
as my good neighbor, sandalfooted, carrying a basket
I am to fill with whatever is too heavy for me to carry.
Your long jowls would force a concentration
should you speak; your ears are pointed in
a ritual of listening, your hair
painted on (he hadn't any, or much), your martial
jacket crossing below your heart, your heart
exposed in the bare beginnings of womanly flesh
old men tend towards in the breast region
—a good reminder that they have hearts.

It must be spring where you come from: you're wearing
cool dress. Still, there is that impatience
of concern about it which reminds me of
my neighbor and professor, who once, I thought
in a snowstorm, needed digging out, except
that he'd jumped from his bedroom window long before
I could climb over the fence to his house
and discover the form of his body impressed in snow,
the footsteps that began out of nothing,
the door sealed up front and back with snow.
I'd seen him praying just the other evening.
Now, with a sense of trespass, I turned home,
then saw him coming towards me, laying down
a slim row of dainty footsteps, bent
forward under the burden of his bookbag
—the mailman it seemed at first, but he was calling out to no one:
*I went to class and not one bloody son of a bitch
showed up,* and laughing, as I was. Whether he saw me
I didn't know for sure, but thought how brilliantly
the street looked after him, a wise man,
well able to care for himself.

You move over low green foothills, swamps
that give no evidence of your having been there.
I imagine the Chinese laborers, true
to each other in form, are very silent when it comes to you.
For you are a good neighbor to them, a monk
full of retiring passions, yet not too full
to take the world beyond and move it inward,
filling your basket with a lexicon of deeds and nature.
The journey you must be on seems full of sorrow.

First Child Married
A Letter Written at the Height of Summer

I am sitting just downhill and lakeward of where
you were married. My body, bent at its two hinges,
and folded up, so held about the knees,
is a triangle, a small pyramid,
while ceaselessly skyward the birches rise up in their own
figure of angles; and the double-barrelled oak is so much
taller than I am; behind me, the woods go on schemeless.
This form is limited.   Still, it is just
as it might be, sketched over the continent, two oceans,
were it describing my arms' shadows, should
each arm reach halfway around the world, East
and West, and meet the obstacle of your island.

Howard is cutting the grass now in strips
of gathering brightness. But he's left the yellow mums
ringed by a thin fortress of grass—a moat
with the sun full on it. And there are other islands he's circled,
covered in pine mulch and maple, so that the lawn
is an archipelago of smaller provinces,
amazingly blossomed, for which I am thankful. Howard
has not added to his Indian color this summer,
but he has put on weight, and his tattoo is hard to interpret
—no longer a dragon, but not quite a fish either;
now, when his clenched upper vertebrae smooth as he straightens,
each image breaks clean from the mainland, until there are many
bright, independent, no-man's nations
studding the flesh of his back and shoulders, like lush islands.
Besides this, there are only four white chairs
left facing the absence of a table; and backed in a corner
of the terrace, the white chaise, looking for all
the world bereft as a parent. It is hard to throw off
the image of myself there: mother to those four white chair-
shaped children, to whom I'd read aloud your letters
while Howard went on in silent contemplation
of the depths beneath his plowshares.

And I am surprised by this inspiration of fondness
for him, by the real affection I feel for those serious
chairs on the terrace; by all that I now feel
that I did not feel in my first marriage.

Were there really three hundred witnesses to your marriage?
And did you really look so pale and prim?
Ah, sweetheart, you never were any good at dissembling,
and wore your jib-white sail from father to husband.
So like you, that movement, that smooth passage yielding
no surrender nor promise! Here, pretending to be
the Mother of Egypt, in whose infinite vision all things
are equal, I try to remember the toasts, the glasses
breaking for me on this same terrace, but the grass,
so very trim and soft and green now, makes
a terrible difference between us:

                                    with fall just perceptible,
the lake so full of wind that it wobbles,
forgive me for filling up the silence with image
upon image: you see, while the light is falling through holes
in the woods, or swarming up the trees as pollen
drifts between the two poles, superimposed
again and again on the branches, the image of water,
the indefatigable mums double
in the grass like clover, but the grass is printed with huge
transparencies: French doors more elegant
than you ever wanted, doors the height of summer,
or, as I've always imagined summer is
at its tail-end, for a child without a mother,
a mother childless—now for you, on your island.

To Atlas in the Attic

Stored in the attic, even in sleep
—dust-covered, greening, a careless package
underneath the eaves—the world
still clings to you, your thoughtless body.
Statue, what tale will you teach my children
at night as they climb to the attic to hide,
and hold you for the first time seeking history?

How long have you lain on your side, and is it
more peaceful there? You, who had glory
and speech: Aratus, Theocritus, all
Alexandria mourned you, though you are merely
a myth to me, once displayed
in sunlight. I read then on your burning back
the shape of things: continents, seas,
tracing and turning the map. Bronze man,
you would have cast the world aside
if you could, had you dared. But oh, from May
to November, given the world to endure,
only your size was certain; and patience
was given a meaning: the lasting shrug
of your shoulder blazed beneath the sky,
the bronze beads like tears rising.

The day you fell headlong from
your pedestal, had you decided
to split the pain, like open pages;
see the soldered globe returned
like melon at your feet? You toppled almost
innocently. Now only
a bronze head remains, your image
lonely, gracing the living room.

"Quite good," some say, but in passing. You
were the world. World-wide you were
renamed, remade. Once you became

a mountain. But whether of stone or plaster
always upholding the greater creation.

To a child the earth is a mystery,
like you a statue, or a round story:
his favorite fruit with neither bruise
nor fragrance like the orchard fruit
you carried home to Heracles
from the far Hesperides. And though sorrow
is everlasting, and heaven recedes,
your strong palms turned upwards still
move me to childish belief,
bearing the gift of the night sky
where every star is named by you.

A Pleasure

For your birthday, three deer appeared
just like that, as if you'd wished
to wake up to the unexpected.

And yet wasn't there the sense
of having known it all (you said)
already; isn't that what pleasure is?

Oh, a simple thought, perhaps,
no more complex than turning seventy
should you be so lucky; no, nor than

the deer themselves, turning up
so close to us the day will always be
—you know, like Frost's—the day we saw the deer

who had, at least so far, lost nothing
to their own adventuring.

Preparing to Move

For a long time, we sit
at home and watch the evening
fall on the brick in the backyard,

the plum-colored shade of the round
table full of holes
dropping its disks of light

onto the anthills. There are drifts
in the garden, pale as hayseed:
a wasting of tulips and jonquils,

a blonde basket of gloves,
the sodden two-by-fours
and tools left over by the fence,

and the soil around the dogwood
is a bare island,
pocked by rain and cherry pits.

We guess at what this or that
depression will yield, come August,
at what will become of the nest

balanced on the egg end
of the lamp in the garage
—a hatful of damp feathers

the wind rocks, and lifts
as if spiriting the nest
away in pieces, now

that we have looked in and touched it—
like the quiet drift
of houses that the black

columns of ants carry with them;
or like this exchange
of light for shadow   that travels

over their dark roads,
and over the hull of the bell
still hanging from the dogwood,

over each cropped branch
until it is the same
shy grey as those feathers,

almost like the cold
that is beginning to reach us:
the white shock of the moon

over the terrace, that touches
down as if it had
nowhere else to go,

that touches the flowers just barely
so that they seem to be steering the darkness
by their own breath.

Notes

The opening epigraph of part 1 is from Blaise Pascal, *Pensées,* translated by A. J. Krailsheimer (Harmondsworth, England: Penguin, 1966), 59. Reproduced by permission of Penguin Books Ltd.

"Living Here": The epigraph is from Robert Frost, "New Hampshire," in *The Poetry of Robert Frost,* edited by Edward Connery Lathem (New York: Holt, Rinehart & Winston, 1963). Reprinted by permission of the Estate of Robert Frost, Jonathan Cape Ltd., and Henry Holt and Company.

"Suicidio": The epigraph is from Eugenio Montale, *Ossi di seppia* (Milan: Arnoldo Mondadori, 1948), 47. Copyright © 1948, 1949, 1957 by Arnoldo Mondadori Editore. Reprinted by permission of New Directions Publishing Corporation. November 4 was the date of the 1918 Italian victory over the Austro-Hungarian army in World War I; on the same date in 1966, Florence suffered a flood that seriously damaged much of the artwork of the city and thwarted plans for the construction of a modern bridge over the Arno and for additional reconstruction of those bridges destroyed by German mines in 1944.

"American Patriotic": The italicized words are from Stephen Vincent Benét, *John Brown's Body,* IV.vi.1.34, in *The Selected Works of Stephen Vincent Benét* (New York: Holt, Rinehart & Winston, 1937). Copyright, 1937, by Stephen Vincent Benét. Copyright renewed © 1964 by Thomas C. Benét, Stephanie C. Mahin, and Rachel Benét Lewis. Reprinted by permission of Brandt & Brandt Literary Agents, Inc.